About the Author

Shikha Chaudhry is an engineer by training, an entrepreneur by profession, and a writer by heart. A graduate of Cornell University, she now runs her own company in India. She takes a lot of pride in her contradictions – she is logical but idealist, a passionate music lover who is tone deaf, and a practical dreamer. On most days, she thinks she can fly. On the rest of the days, she works on her undone wings. Her family and loved ones are her biggest strength.

Hacking Happiness

Shikha Chaudhry

Hacking Happiness

Olympia Publishers
London

www.olympiapublishers.com
OLYMPIA PAPERBACK EDITION

Copyright © Shikha Chaudhry 2024

The right of Shikha Chaudhry to be identified as author of this work has been asserted in accordance with sections 77 and 78 of the Copyright, Designs and Patents Act 1988.

All Rights Reserved

No reproduction, copy or transmission of this publication may be made without written permission.
No paragraph of this publication may be reproduced, copied or transmitted save with the written permission of the publisher, or in accordance with the provisions of the Copyright Act 1956 (as amended).

Any person who commits any unauthorized act in relation to this publication may be liable to criminal prosecution and civil claims for damage.

A CIP catalogue record for this title is available from the British Library.

ISBN: 978-1-80439-770-1

The opinions expressed in this book are the author's own and do not reflect the views of the publisher, author's employer, organisation, committee or other group or individual.

First Published in 2024

Olympia Publishers
Tallis House
2 Tallis Street
London
EC4Y 0AB

Printed in Great Britain

Dedication

I dedicate this book to my three nephews.

Prologue

When I decided to write about happiness, I knew I was directly competing with Buddha. Nonetheless, I took up the challenge as I believe the world can be a much happier place. While Buddha was enlightened, I am entitled – entitled to my opinions, anyway.

This book is a reflection of my limited experiences, and rather narrow viewpoints. I am privileged to be born in a family where the only real struggle while growing up was to score good grades. I believe I lead a happy life, surrounded by people I absolutely love. Most of the chapters in this book are based on those people and their shortcomings.

The biggest reason for my happiness is my parents – I can't thank them enough for their love, encouragement, and support. My mother is the strongest woman I know, and has always taught me to work hard (which I do) and have a positive outlook (which I don't). I am also incredibly lucky to have two loving siblings, whom I always find by my side.

My brother, who is optimistic to a fault, encouraged me to write this book and made me believe someone would be willing to read it. And, his wife, who is not so optimistic, played the perfect role of a taskmaster. Thanks, you two.

I am also fortunate that I find immense happiness in my work; purpose and goals can wait.

Last but not the least, my loving partner ensures that I live a peaceful and fairly happy life, on most days. Everyone can use a little love!

Happiness

Everyone wants to be happy, nobody knows how to be. If you ask people what makes them happy, the answers are surprisingly generic. And if you ask them what they are doing to become happier, most people fumble. If the ultimate aim is to lead a happy life, why don't we actively and deliberately pursue happiness? Why don't we hear about happiness hacks, like the way they talk about productivity hacks, money saving hacks, even life hacks? Most importantly, why can't we train our mind to practice happiness?

Like most precious things in life, happiness does not come naturally, on its own. We must chase it relentlessly, find it somehow, and work on it thoughtfully. That said, it is not a mathematical theorem, nothing can keep you happy forever. It is the sum total of many things, things that will keep changing over time. You have to keep pace with its dynamism. And, there is no one-size-fits-all solution. Happiness means different things to different people, it means different things to the same people at different times. It is not a single point, but a whole range.

Like your thoughts and actions, only you are responsible for your happiness. It is nobody else's imperative, but your own pursuit. You just can't delegate it to others. People around you may amplify your happiness levels, and/or share your happiness, but the burden (or lack of it) to make yourself happy lies with you. Being happy is a promise that you have to make to yourself. You may not always be able to keep it, but trying it is a choice only you can make.

Know that happiness is not a myth. It is a skill that can be developed, it is a muscle that can be built, and it is an artifact that can be hacked. This book is an attempt to enumerate the factors that can help you score happiness, and how there can be a step-by-step approach to improving your happiness levels. Genetically, there are some of us who are prone to unhappiness. Fate plays a huge role too. This book conspicuously misses out on such harsh realities. It simply challenges some of the preconceived notions, and offers "practical philosophy" for a slightly privileged person.

Myth 1: Money Can't Buy Happiness

Chase Materialistic Things

Money is what money does. If spending it gives you happiness, consider it well invested. You can't decide that you don't love a fancy watch till you own a couple of them, you can't live in the bubble that a luxurious car is a wasteful buy until your garage houses at least one, you can't write off a fancy house unless you own one. Drop the pretense, chase these materialistic things, buy some of them in your 30s and 40s, and renounce them in your 50s. Know that you have to own them now to renounce them later.

Money is also like love, it has to be experienced. Travel far and wide while you are young and fit, collect moments, and frame them. The view is always better from a yacht, don't hesitate if that view is costly. A private beach can lighten up your head, don't worry if it lightens the wallet too. Buy all the experiences you possibly can. At some point, they may seem more valuable than the interest on that fixed deposit. At that point, when you are old and wrinkly, travel a bit more and buy more experiences.

Money is a tool, use it however you like. If your purpose is to pursue pleasure, and you work hard to indulge in grandeur, it does not make you a shallow being. Happiness does not always lie in glorified, larger-than-life aims; hedonism is but a form of happiness. But make sure it is your hard-earned money. It won't be half as fulfilling an experience if you didn't earn it first. Create measurable goals, achieve them, strike off your to-buy list and live a life of luxury.

All this comes with a catch, though. Remember that you are neither doing it for vanity, nor do you want a debt-full life. You are doing it because earning money is as fun as spending it, you are doing it for your intrinsic happiness. It is arguably a thin line. If you don't make it thick enough, you are bound to falter. You will spiral into a circle of inadequacy with a force greater than your fast car's torque.

That said, don't let anyone tell you money can't buy happiness, try it first-hand to establish what works for you. You can always use that 50-inch plasma TV for magnificence in your 40s, and for self-reflection in your 50s.

Build a Lavish Home

You must commit to a place, and earnestly plan to build your dream house in your lifetime – the sooner, the better. If it falls short, be happy with your very real "aim house." Don't think of your house as an investment, that's what investments are for. Your house is much more than that – it is an emotion, a promise, your eternal imperfection, and your constant. It grows with you.

Find your *literal* happy place, make it happier. Call it home, and nurture it like a baby.

Home may mean different things to different people, but it makes most of us happy and content even if the equations vary.

Equation One: Home = Walls + Story
Hidden and safe behind those walls, every home has its own unique story. Home is where you matter, your stories matter, where you start your journey from and come back to, after all the wanderings. It is your safe sanctuary – make your walls thick, and your story endearing.

Equation Two: Home = Habitat + Life
Every animal needs a habitat – an environment where they get water, food, shelter, and comfortable space. Home is your habitat where life happens, it is a place that meets your needs – tangible and intangible. It is your state of mind – it must be stable, well-balanced and peaceful.

Equation Three: Home = Structure + People
The purpose of a home is to keep the outside world out, and the

inside world in. Home is a place which is never empty, where you don't crave for your own space, where boisterous noises are a norm. It is your creation – the beams and columns make it strong, and people make it stronger.

Equation Four: Home = House + Love
The functional aspect is as important as the emotional bit. Home is what you keep building, inch by inch, memory by memory, day in and out. It is a work in progress – there is always a way to make it more pretty, and there is always a way to make it more cozy.

You know you are home, when you are home. Home is a place where you are always right.

Myth 2: Choose to be Optimistic

Not Optimists, but *Hopeists* Would Win the Day

An optimist is a person who falls from the 15th floor of a building and claims they are happy it wasn't 16th. A pessimist is someone who never climbs the building for fear of falling off. Both invalidate an authentic human experience – the latter for not trying, former for trying so hard.

Facts don't matter to an optimist, only prospects do. They expect things to fall in place, the *glass* to always be full. An optimist lives under the constant burden of ignoring the darkness, seeing the light out of every tunnel for everyone around them, while a pessimist is never willing to acknowledge the brightness in their own backyard. A pessimist rarely expects, since they inherently know their glass is not full, they don't bother to check it or fill it. Both have their own demons to fight.

An optimist is adamant to see the positives in every situation that the truth stops mattering to them; a pessimist is busy worrying in every situation that they stop chasing the truth. Both see a rather distorted version of reality.

The world disproportionately values optimistic values. Every quote, every leader, every self-help book nudges you to become an optimist. An optimist is expected to grab every single opportunity like a superhuman, and take the world forward. Misplaced optimism is, however, fatal. At the very least, it causes misery because life has its own way of showing the truth.

Now, if someone just removes their rose-colored glasses and

looks around, they will see a *hopeist* with equally tinted glasses but with an umbrella – an umbrella the optimist thinks they will never need, an umbrella the pessimist is never willing to put back.

A hopeist hopes for the sunshine, while being prepared for the storm. They make no assumption that everything will turn out fine, they believe they can act to make things work. They certainly hope to fly while being mindful of the fact that they have to hone their wings. And, when they fall, they get up, check their bruises, and learn to nurse them.

In one 2004 paper in the *Journal of Social and Clinical Psychology*, two psychologists asserted that "hope focuses more directly on the personal attainment of specific goals; whereas, optimism focuses more broadly on the expected quality of future outcomes in general."

And, in hope lies their happiness. Hopeists know the world has no obligation to make them happy, they believe in their own capabilities to set things right. They hope, not expect. They act, not assume.

In conclusion, hope is something you do, optimism/pessimism is an attitude. You can be hopeless but optimistic; hopeful but pessimistic or hopeful and optimistic.

Be that as it may, but always choose hope and then practice it for life.

Myth 3: Patience Is a Virtue

Patience Could be a Virtue, Impatience Is a Blessing

If life is short, how can you afford to be patient? Even worse, how can you let procrastination win over life?

Run out of patience, throw away your procrastination, and rush toward your dream. Good things don't come to people who wait, but to those who make them happen.

To live a fulfilling life though, you don't have to do extraordinary stuff on a daily basis, but ordinary things regularly. Show up at work every day, put your blinkers on, and embrace boring routines. Somewhere in those repetitive, banal routines lies your future success. You just have to follow them. Chase consistency, not perfection. Humans are anyway not meant to be perfect.

Following a routine does not mean you have to be patient. Be impatiently patient – impatient to work every day, but patient to do the same thing over and over till you achieve desired results. And, when you achieve what you set out to do, don't call it a day. Move the goalpost, and start working toward that. Be very impatient, never accept the status quo! Impatience may not be a virtue but it can be a damn blessing. It gets things done.

Be as it were, but never take it slow. Those who are not in a hurry reach nowhere. There must not be speed limits on the road to success, at least not the self-created ones. Go as far as life permits. Never let patience slow you down.

Your life is a sum total of your actions – big and small. And, success seems to be connected with actions. Keep moving! Cover some distance, and record some displacement. Results can take their own sweet time, but your actions must not.

How will this make you happy, you ask? Well, success is the companionate lover of happiness. Success may not always be sufficient for happiness, but it's necessary.

Side note: Reserve all your impatience for yourself though. Don't be impatient with people or a situation, know that you can't control either. You can perhaps change one person, but not people in general. You can probably control the direction of your life, but not its moments. Concentrate on micros when dealing with people, and macros when dealing with life.

Be Patient with People Though, Delay That Reaction

Between the time an incident that demands your reaction occurs and the time when you actually react, lies your peace. Maximize it.

For every action, there is an equal and opposite reaction, Newton has taught us. In real life, the equation is slightly extended. For every impulsive reaction, there is an equal or more regret.

Action -> Reaction -> Regret -> Unhappiness

In most situations, your unhappiness is inversely proportional to your reaction time, and directly related to your regrets. The more you delay your reaction time, the less would be the intensity of your reaction, the less would be the regret and the more will be your happiness quotient.

The idea is to change the equation by adding sufficient delay:

Action -> Reaction + Delay -> Less Regret -> Happiness

And if you must react, react without a reaction. "Choose the non-emotional response to any given situation and see how much easier your life becomes," Naval Ravikant says.

Action -> Reaction + Delay – Emotions -> (Very) Less

Regret -> (More) Happiness

Adding an adequate amount of delay and reducing enough emotions won't be simple. It will need practice and consideration. Deliberately add ten minutes before you respond to that Slack message, or that provocative email or even that personal confrontational discussion. From real time communication, make it (real + delta) time communication. During that delta time, remove all the emotions from your response.

This does not mean you stop acting though. Great things happen to those who can't wait and are always in action mode. Act on your own accord by all means, just don't let a situation/person make you react. No one should have that kind of power on you. But, if someone does have that power, acknowledge that they are special, and that this equation would fail. The trick is to keep the number of such people as small as possible.

Act fast, react late should be the mantra. How late depends on you and only you.

Myth 4: Enjoy the Journey, Destination Will Come

Nothing Succeeds Like Success

Everything in life comes in the shades of grey, except winning and losing. That is in black and white. The sound of victory is never mistaken for a cry of defeat, by anyone. They are remarkably distinct.

Winning may not guarantee peace, but losing hardly ever makes anyone happy. You can't always fall back on the enriched experience you gained after losing, there are only so many times, so many things you can learn after losing. Eventually, you need to hear the sound of victory.

So, you have two choices:
a) Play to win
b) Or, don't play at all.

There is merit in choosing inaction. If you can train yourself to tread on that tedious path of detachment where winning and losing does not matter, you already are a winner. However, for the vast majority, the choice does not always lie with them. Modern life, much like a war, nudges you to play. Then, why not play harder and make winning a habit?

Make no mistake though, stochastically speaking, you can't always win. You *will* not always win. But you can choose to work hard to win. You can choose to put in your best efforts, you can choose to dream to win, and you can choose to work even harder to remain a winner, when you eventually win. Victory, after all, lies in not getting defeated.

A winner is someone who refuses to lose, who tries the hardest, and who believes in fair play. A happy winner is someone who loves to win more than they hate to lose.

Play to win every battle in life, except arguments. Be humble to admit that you are wrong, and change your mind when you are wrong. Smart people, anyway, change their minds often. Some may call you wishy-washy, but you will be at peace. You will save some energy, you will also make your loved ones think they are right (even if you secretly know they are not).

You can do this, in the pursuit of happiness.

Sweat in the Journey, Stay Busy, and be Happy

Find the things that you love, and get so busy living that you don't have time to be unhappy. But you don't have to fill your life with barren busyness, instead the key is to find relevant and enjoyable tasks.

> Irrelevant + Enjoyable = Meaningless
> Relevant + Non-enjoyable = Unhappiness
> Irrelevant + Non-enjoyable = Doesn't need to be answered

Explore, sprint, rest, repeat.

Establishing what you love and find fun is arguably not a simple task. You need to be extremely self-aware, you should also have the guts to discard what you don't want to do, and you have to be always thinking.

There is a hack, though.

There are two fail-safe ways to find what is fun for you:

a) Go back to the time when you were eight, and list down what was fun then. If you wanted to do it then, chances are you still want to do them, but with an adult filter.

b) Or come back to the present and think of all the things you are envious about. You are jealous because you find them fun, but are not able to do them.

Admittedly, this is a rather loosely described definition of fun. But, before we discuss that, know that you don't have to be a *fun apologist*. Don't let anyone (yourself included) tell you fun is a diversion from a successful life. You can have fun and still be successful, you can have fun and still be an adult, you can have fun and still be taken seriously. You just have to redefine fun!

Fun is not synonymous to being flaky, abandoning responsibilities or refusing to grow up. Don't fall into the trap of fleeting fun, which neither requires much effort nor is it worth going after. You don't have to put in efforts to have a drunken night with friends, for instance. It is pleasurable while it lasts, and it does not last long. This lifestyle could be seductive, but is hardly meaningful. Purposeful fun with mindfulness, on the other hand, is joyful, permanent and transcendental.

Figure out your destination and make the journey fun.

Myth 5: Believe in Yourself, Know Your Power

Outsource Self-Belief

If self-belief is a key to success, outsourcing that belief to a bunch of important people in your life is the key to happiness. That way, whenever you run low on belief, they can refill your quota. Let's call it shared belief.

For that to happen, you have to first accept that you can't do it all. You are not a magnetic train, you are not self-sustainable day in and day out. With this realization in place, you must find and develop your tribe. You can choose them from your inner circle (Reference: *Invest in all your relationships*). Think of them as your charging stations. They should be your cheerleaders and your *mirror-holders* – when you are in doubt, they should cheer you; and when you don't see the reality, they must show you the mirror. You need both kinds. This is a critical first step, you must be sure of the people you are giving this kind of control to. Neither do you want an echo chamber, nor a room full of negative energy.

The second step is to believe in what they say when you approach them in your downtime, without questioning them. You can't be selective here, you can't cherry-pick good parts from the bad ones. If you have made them a part of your shared belief system, you don't get to put terms and conditions. In any case, if you have done the first step right, you may not even have the need to question them.

Finally, you should return the favor too, you should also be a part of someone else's tribe. It is relatively simpler to pump in others, as compared to charging up yourself.

Evidently, you will give some people a lot of power in your life and it may sound opposite to conventional wisdom, but it is a practical approach, with a tinge of *hopeism*. It will also take some burden off you. A lighter mind is the step toward a happy mind.

P.S.: Don't make your parents a part of your tribe, they can never be objective about you. Your partner, who loves and tolerates you in equal parts, should be a good choice. If they are not, you may have bigger problems!

Know Your Limits, Mindfully Ignore Them

In a world where knowledge is touted as the biggest weapon, "mindfully ignoring" i.e. ignoring the things you can't control is the step toward peace and happiness. That is real knowledge. Wake up to your limitations, embrace them even. But don't let them stop you from taking action.

How can we train our mind to ignore, though? Let's understand from three examples.

Example 1: Think of an oncologist, she understands human anatomy, fixes the cancerous cells, while knowing fully well they may come back and she won't be able to do anything. That does not stop her from treating her patients.

Lesson: Try everything in your power to fix a gigantic problem, still accept that you won't be able to find solutions to, sometimes, even a small problem at your own home. Accept that your action may not always yield results, but try as hard as you possibly can. Have a bias toward action, but mindfully relinquish control. Ignore the end result.

Example 2: Think of a fighter plane pilot, he fights for a living, faces fear like no one else, but does not let it impact his judgment. He knows he has to fight/live in the moment, quite literally, he still makes strategies for the future.

Lesson: Know that hearts break, marriages fail, businesses go kaput, still make plans for forever. Mindfully, accept all things that may go wrong to plan for a future that may turn out right. Plan for a future, but tell your mind to live in the moment. Ignore uncertainties on the way.

Example 3: Think of a baby, when you throw him up in the air playfully, he believes you will catch him every single time. He trusts you, feels comfortable with you. He is not scared, shocked, or worried. On your part, you never break his trust.

Lesson: You can't always have all the answers. Trust the universe, it will invariably lead you in the right direction. As an experienced adult, you are bound to be skeptical. Try losing parts of it every day, and mindfully learn to believe in the goodness of people around you. Ignore your brain's cynicism.

While you are trying to find peace of mind, you may achieve peace from mind. That's not half bad a deal.

Myth 6: Best Relationships are Effortless

Invest in All Your Relationships

Everyone, after a certain age, is advised to invest their savings wisely. And, if you are reasonably smart, your diverse investments in traditional investment tools will certainly reap you long-term benefits. With that same sharpness of mind (and heart), you should invest in your relationships – with your friends, colleagues, siblings, parents, partner, pets, and kids, in no particular order.

The first step is to pick the people who matter to you, and put them in your inner circle. Narrowly diversify that group, you don't have to go wide! Always try to keep them happy. Start by saying yes (judiciously) to them. A pilgrim holiday? *Yes, Mom, let's do it.* This TV series over that? *Sure, why not.* A pottery class? *Of course.* Meet my parents this weekend? *No, I am not ready for that.* You don't have to be a pushover, but flexible for small and big things.

Second, always think long-term when investing your time, energy, and emotions. Go long, and choose value investing. "Only buy something that you'd be perfectly happy to hold if the market shut down for ten years," says Warren Buffett. The same holds true for relationships.

The third attribute is earnestness. You can't invest fake money and expect it to grow; similarly, you can't put fake emotions in a real relationship.

Finally, be mindful that all investments are subject to market risks. Not every bet of yours will hedge, not every investment will yield results, not every relationship will be fruitful. If you live long enough, you will see your fair share of heartbreaks, broken friendships, and struggling relationships.

Relationships are beautiful. You don't live on an island, know that people make you happy. What you should practice though is, they should not make you sad. That part of your life's control should stay with you. Otherwise, you will be in an emotional prison.

That being said, you can't let your relationships define the whole of you and you can't live your life through others. Write your song, find your tribe, dance it out with them, try and match their rhythm. If ultimately the music does not seem right, dare to be your own person.

Love Needs Tremendous Work

The best feeling in the world is to be loved, the only thing that can top it is to find someone you love. When you find that *someone*, hold on to them. But till the time you don't, keep looking. You have to keep giving chances to love, you have to believe in the miracle of love and you shouldn't try to explain love – it has to be cellular-level deep. In the process of finding love, you will get your heart broken. Don't give up! We can learn to love only by loving. "Have enough courage to trust love one more time and always one more time," Maya Angelou rightfully said.

Falling in love is, however, simple, staying in love isn't. Falling in love is natural, staying in love needs practice and discipline. Falling in love is effortless, staying in love requires tons of work. Falling in love is biology, staying in love is civil engineering – you have to keep the pieces together. Falling in love is compulsive, staying in love is a choice. Always choose to stay in love. Don't give up!

Love should feel like home, an anchor, a shelter – warm, sturdy and slightly boring. You may notice some cracks when it gets old, repair them when you see them. Be relieved that you don't have to build it all over again. If the passage bores you, know that it once gave you comfort. Take solace in the fact that it is not an unfamiliar alley. Paint it, decorate it, add some artifacts – it will become rusty and old. It will become you!

The effect of love on humans is undeniable. A life full of love is a happy life, and love takes many forms. According to the triangular theory of love, developed by Robert Sternberg, the three components of love are an intimacy component, a passion component, and a decision/commitment component. Start from wherever, but end at the companionate love – a love that features intimacy and commitment, and is based less on passionate highs and lows, a love low on fanciness but high on friendship, a love that is an afterglow.

When you love as well as *like* that person, when that person brings out the best in you, when you both are looking in the same direction, when love and laughter coincide, when you have your soul intact but can share it with a mate, when your mind is peaceful, that is when you are in companionate love – the only source of true happiness. Come for passion, stay for companionship.

If you don't know how to love though, get a dog and learn from him. He demands your attention, but reciprocates. He is clingy, but faithful. He is stubborn, but forgiving. He senses everything, but never doubts.

Be a dog in your relationship, happiness will follow.

To Have or Not to Have?

Do you sometimes miss the rewind button in life? Perhaps, you could go back in time and enjoy the experiences you couldn't while growing up – learn guitar, a new language, scuba training, spend more time near the ocean, see the world with a different lens. Or do you feel cheated that, try as you may, you can't keep believing in magic after you hit a certain age? Do you miss being less cynical? Do you want your curiosity back?

Life gives you another chance, that button if you may, when you decide to have kids. You can relive your life with your kids, this time certainly more custom-made. It is also an opportunity to right the wrongs or wrong the rights, depending on your vantage point.

By no stretch of imagination, raising a kid is easy. And, for this generation (people born after 1980), it will always be a *what if* scenario. If you choose to have kids, you may wonder what life would have been without them. If you decide not to have kids, you may wonder what life would have been with them. Damned if you do, damned if you don't. On one hand, you get plenty of free time, quality sleep, scrumptious brunches, fat bank balance, impromptu travels, on the other, you sign up for crazy days, sleepless nights, rushed meals, not-so-fat bank balance, impromptu cuddles. The equation is awfully asymmetric. Still take your chances, it is rewarding.

Kids give you purpose, and snatch away all your free time to be morose. In the initial years, they demand so much of your time and energy that you forget about sadness, your life becomes a treadmill; in the long term, they, rather unwittingly, nudge you to become a better person. You don't want to fail in their eyes, hence you try harder to be successful, happy, and resilient. You also learn selflessness as you start loving a human being more than you love yourself. All the centrifugal and centripetal forces are toward them, and they realign the center of your life. Physics fails, as much as logic, when you decide to have and raise kids. Still go for it, it is adventurous.

Are parents happier than childless couples? A study from Princeton University and Stony Brook University found "very little difference" between the life satisfaction of parents and nonparents, but parents experienced both more daily joy and stress than nonparents. Parents, in general, also experience more irrational fear, paranoia and anxiety. "Making the decision to have a child—it is momentous. It is to decide forever to have your heart go walking around outside your body," educator Elizabeth Stone said. Still choose to become a parent, it is a privilege.

Kids are your dream come true, dreams you didn't even know you dreamt (*conditions apply*).

A (Fur) Bowl Full of Mush

Say, you are in a messed-up mood and you want to be left alone. You crave for your space and just want to melt slowly. But there is this one friend who would never let you be. They know you are in a dark space, they also understand your need to be alone, but they still won't leave your side. You can fight with them, yell at them but they won't budge. Deep inside though, you love that they are there for you. They are your best friend, always have been.

Say, you come home after a long day at work, you don't want to discuss anything, don't want to return any calls, you quite like the silence of the night. You just want to snuggle in a blanket with your partner, along with a hot cup of tea. You love that warmth, and you want to hold on to it. Perhaps, that is the only touch you need at that moment – your partner in that cuddly blanket.

Say, you faced a humongous failure, no one trusts your judgment any more. Even you yourself doubt your capability. The only cheerleaders left in your life, at that particular instance, are your parents. They are oblivious to your failures, you can't ever be a loser for them. They may not give you a pep talk, you don't even want it, but the look in their eyes tells you that they believe in you. You are forever their star!

Say, you are in a playful mood for no apparent reason. You want to prance around, be a child all over again. Some days are like that. The only person you want to share this simpleton joy with is your favorite sibling. Your energy rubs on them, and they get equally charged. You both act silly, jumping and rolling.

There is nowhere else you'd rather be and no one else you'd rather be with. That, right there, is pure unadulterated bliss.

Now, replace your best friend, partner, parents and your sibling with your pet. Your pet never leaves your side, senses your mood to a fault, provides you all the warmth that you need, thinks you are forever their hero, and are fun to be with. If they are not an all-encompassing source of happiness and joy, then who is?

P.S.: Don't actually replace humans with your dog/pet, just bring the ball of fur into your life for that extra pinch of happiness. They hug with their eyes!

Make Room for...Yourself

You are ambitious, you don't always know what you want to achieve. Both can be true.
You are super disciplined, you sometimes don't have it under control. Both can be true.
You are self-reliant, you want someone to have your back. Both can be true.
You take big risks, you are scared to death. Both can be true.
You have a drive to excel, you want to laze around. Both can be true.
You love your kids, you enjoy and crave for your *me time*. Both can be true.
You have a huge paycheck, you need someone's help to do your taxes. Both can be true.
You are pretty outspoken, you can't say no to people. Both can be true.
You are authentic to the world, you don't mind some disingenuity with yourself. Both can be true.
You have thick skin, you are vulnerable. Both can be true.
You have figured it out, you don't have all the answers. Both can be true.
You have a calming demeanor, there is a storm brewing inside. Both can be true.
You are decisive, you need someone's help to choose your meals. Both can be true.
You always take charge, you want to relinquish all control. Both can be true.
You are a leader, you want someone to show you the right way.

Both can be true.

True happiness lies in embracing these dichotomies. Accept that your life is ruled by these contrasting, sharply different forces and that you can't always be consistent. Tolerate your somewhat erratic behavior, cut some slack for that person in the mirror. The world has not been designed to be navigated via a straight line, it's always going to be chaotic. You must make room for yourself and your contradictions.

If you contradict yourself, it makes you pretty intelligent, in an insane kind of way. And, since you are not trying to fix it, it is bound to make you happy, or at least content.

Myth 7: Live a Purposeful Life

Life Can Be a Vacation

According to the Merriam-Webster dictionary, vacation comes from Latin: vacātiōn-, vacātiō means "exemption from service, respite from work," and traces back to vacāre, "to be empty, be free, and have leisure." And, the earliest known example of vacation occurs in Geoffrey Chaucer's fourteenth century book *The Canterbury Tales*. This leads to two quick conclusions:
    a) Taking a vacation is certainly not a new phenomenon, it is not a by-product of *work-life no balance* lifestyle. Even simpletons with non-crappy bosses wanted a break.
    b) Taking a vacation increases the happiness quotient.
    The pertinent question is why. Why do we need a vacation? Why do we have to travel to get sunburned? Why do we have to be at a beach to break the monotony? Why don't we watch the sunsets from our balconies when we are not on a vacation? Why can't we find majestic, exotic where we are? If we have to escape, are we in the prison then? Who created it for us? And, how do we break free, given our contours and boundaries?
    The answer requires both introspection and calculated actions.
    We should not keep craving for a vacation, rather find the reasons that stop our life from becoming a vacation. More often than not, the barriers are self-created.
    Where you live (your literal happy place), whom you live with (invest in all your relationships) and what you do for a living (play to win) deterministically explain if your life can be modeled to become a vacation. Remember the three Ps: place, people and

profession. The good part is you can control, choose and change all three, if you wish to. The bad part is you can't offload this tedious work to anyone else, only you can figure out what works for you. And the combination won't be right in the first attempt, either. It will require multiple iterations.

Know that even if all your Ps are robust, you will still want an occasional break, you will yearn for an environment of nothingness, you will cherish that tan. Sunsets will look prettier from the deck, the exotic will be hard to find, and high tides will bring better vibes. Even simpletons used to go on holidays, remember?

The hack, however, is to build our life in a way that we want to come back to it from an awesome vacation. Life, much like a memorable vacation, starts slowly and ends abruptly. Make the most of it!

Humor It Up

Historically, the term humor referred to the bodily fluid of an animal. Hippocrates is usually credited with applying this idea to medicine. He named the four humors as black bile, phlegm, yellow bile, and blood – they were used to analyze a person's physical, mental, and even emotional health. Back then, medical practitioners used to treat the patients by restoring the balance of these humors.

Science evolved, humor stayed.

Whether laughter is therapeutic or not, it is still considered the best medicine, and not for nothing. Anyone can laugh, as a matter of fact, humans start laughing as early as three months into life, long before they learn how to speak. No one teaches babies how to laugh. Laughter is spontaneous, oftentimes contagious, doesn't have an accent, plays an important role in social bonding, and is a hallmark of great friendships. You don't fake laughter, the only exception being an uncomfortable situation with strangers or your boss' joke. Research also says a good sense of humor is one of the most sought-after qualities while finding a partner. When you laugh with your mouth or your eyes, you are invariably happy, at least at that moment, release of endorphins notwithstanding.

Hence, humor should definitely be taken seriously. To score happy moments, either start appreciating humor around you or develop a sense of humor or do both. Humor is very much a skill that, to begin with, can be practiced on self. In fact, self-deprecating humor is as powerful as self-awareness. It is also a safe bet. You can only offend yourself, and then your thick skin can save you from yourself. Quite a circular loop, you'd say. Note that not everyone has a thick skin, hence once you master the self-effacing part, you can make fun of politicians, situations, or your life in general. Life has the best jokes to tell, if you appreciate humor. Laugh it all away, happiness will follow.

As someone said, humor is no joke. It plays a key role in our understanding of the world and its people. It is also important for businesses, societies, and civilizations. You build better bonds, break more barriers, grow as a whole and cultivate more peace if you can laugh together.

Making someone laugh is the greatest power any human being can have. Find that funny bone, keep tickling it. And, everyone enjoys a good joke. Even gods love jokes, life is proof of that.

Happiness Can be Faked

Fake your happiness not to fool others, but to train your mind. Think of your life as a social media feed and yourself as its only viewer. Glorify it to manipulate your brain, make it remember the good things, and filter off the bad experiences.

Even science proves playing mind games (on your mind, anyway) yields results.

A recent research from the University of South Australia confirms that the mere act of smiling, even if it is fake, can trick your mind into being more positive, simply by moving your facial muscles. "In our research we found that when you forcefully practice smiling, it stimulates the amygdala – the emotional center of the brain – which releases neurotransmitters to encourage an emotionally positive state," Dr. Fernando Marmolejo-Ramos, lead researcher and human and artificial cognition expert with UniSA's Center for Change and Complexity in Learning, asserted.

Your brain can change over time, scientists call it neuroplasticity – the ability of the nervous system to change its activity in response to intrinsic or extrinsic stimuli by reorganizing its structure, functions, or connections. In other words, you can deliberately rewire your brain to be happy, and take steps if it refuses to. Feelings follow actions. If you feel your relationship is inadequate, do something grand for your partner. If you briefly resent someone, do something thoughtful for them. If you feel your career is not going anywhere, have an honest conversation with your boss. This strategy, which takes advantage of flexibility of the brain, works well for minor/temporary problems.

Put simply, happiness is all about chemicals – every time a happiness chemical is released, your brain registers what led to it. The trick is to release such chemicals often. Fake it or make it – the brain can't care less. Fake happiness, in many ways, is better than real misery.

There are three caveats though:

a) You don't have to fake your happiness in front of others. This exercise is strictly for yourself, to habituate your brain to happiness so that it starts opting for it when presented with a choice.

b) You should not end up living a delusional life or chasing just highs. Instead, your brain should work toward converting lows to highs.

c) You should not be working too hard for it. That defeats the purpose.

Body, Soul, and Mind Should Be in Harmony (Not a Myth)

Food

Food is as old as life. From being a source of mere sustenance to a part of the current "paradox of plenty," it continues to evolve with humanity. Our ancestors were hunters-gatherers, and we hunt for online takeaway places while gathering coupons. From cooked food to processed items, the food innovation in modern society has largely been centered around convenience. We now live in a world of fatty abundance, sugarcoated with comfort. However, one thing that hasn't changed is food remains a cornerstone for every civilization, every society, every household. It brings people closer. It is also a universal experience, something that is common between all living beings.

That said, not everyone has the same relationship with food, for some it is a source of immense joy, for others it is a means to an end. It is easy to fall in love with food though, and like all great romances, it becomes addictive and irrational before you know it. But if you take it slow, put in enough work, and make the right choices, the relationship becomes healthy and so do you (quite literally!).

The pertinent question is – why should you sacrifice daily happiness for a healthy body in the long term? The tough choices that you opt for today will certainly make your life simple in future. But is it worth the effort? There are no easy answers.

Depending on your vantage point, your body could be a temple or your childhood home. You can either choose to respect it, treat it with dignity, and be mindful of what goes in it or be laid back about it, bask in its comfort, and keep playing until the summer break lasts. Where do you draw the line?

The simplest hack is to pray inside your home, to merge the temple and your home, to make healthy food delicious, and to remove the abundance quotient from your everyday meals. The secret ingredient is restrained indulgence.

You don't want too much on your plate or too much on your mind. Conversely though, modern societies are defined by excesses and stress. The struggle for most of us is around too much, not too less. If you look closely, you will find excesses and stress are interlinked. Hence, by reducing one, you can control the other.

Thick Skin but a Tender Heart

You will always find unhappiness waiting for you on the road to offense. Never take that road, neither as a driver nor as a passenger. A person, who deliberately offends others, ends up crashing and colliding. An offended person, on the other hand, almost always acts up and forgets his way. You don't want to be either. Don't offend anyone, don't take offense from anyone.

Offense is not equivalent to hurt, it is rather its first cousin – related but different. We don't get offended by our loved ones, they can hurt us, bruise us, damage us, or perhaps ruin us. Offense, however, is caused by strangers or quasi strangers.

The root cause of offense is a breach of expectations. True to our unreasonable self, we expect even absolute strangers crossing our paths to follow their lane, and/or accommodate us. But we will always encounter a few violators, we should avoid engaging with them. Their honking should not perturb us, we should let them overtake us.

We anyway live in a time and age where no one really is offense-proof. The world is in a perpetual state of taking offense. In fact, the business model of all social media companies is buying and selling offense. Every algorithm, every interface and every design element is being created to amplify offense. They want you to offend others and get offended. Don't be their engagement metric. Most of all, let there be non-porous walls between your online self and real life.

In any case, forget people, life in itself is pretty offensive. It attacks you, insults you and often does not agree with you. Do you stop living? You must apply the same principle with people.

You have to accept if something offends you, it is nobody else's responsibility but yours. The world will not take corrective actions to mollycoddle you.

If you are not born with a thick skin, develop that membrane and use it more. If your words can offend someone, think from your heart and use your words less. A thick skin with a tender heart is a lethal combination, it takes the power away from everyone and lands it on you. Use it often.

Health

Does happiness improve our physical health, or does good health lead to happiness? How are they correlated? Let's think out loud.

    If you are unwell, do you feel happy? No
    If you are healthy, do you feel happy? Maybe
    If you are happy, does your health improve? Maybe
    If you are unhappy, does it impact your well-being? Yes

Loosely speaking, it proves good health is a prerequisite to achieve happiness. Conversely, if you are unhealthy, you can't be overly happy. A healthy body may not be a source of happiness, but a sick body definitely leads to unhappiness. As Confucius said, "A healthy man wants a thousand things, a sick man only wants one." For you to live a fulfilling life, a content life, a life full of hope, you need to eliminate bad health.

However, scoring good health is neither easy, nor rewarding in the short term. Healthy eating, practicing meditation or hitting the gym require deliberate efforts, with no instant gratification. Junk food, on the other hand, has been scientifically designed to induce satisfaction, albeit temporary. The smell, how it feels in our mouth, the orosensation, and the actual composition of the food make them addictive. So, how do you resist the temptation?

A simple hack to attain good health is to always take *long cuts*. Choose walking over driving, stairs over elevators, cooking over ordering in, reading before you hit the sack over mindless scrolling. Anything which is fast and convenient is simply not healthy. The second hack is to remove friction in choosing these long cuts – they should be effortless. A morning walk is as healthy as an evening stroll. Don't force yourself to wake up early if you are not a morning person. The third hack is to attach them to your chores – walking to supermarkets, if done regularly, is no less effective than walking in a park. That being said, there is no one size fits all solution here. *Pun intended.* Find what works best for you, and be consistent. If it's important, do it every day. If it's not important, don't do it at all, says weightlifting coach and author Dan John.

Finally, note that the health of your loved ones is also your responsibility, your happiness is linked to their health as well. Take that seriously too. Cajole, convince, coach them to maintain good health. Never not interfere!

A healthy body is the best fashion statement. A healthy household is the happiest of them all. You can't demand it, you have to nourish it.

Joy of Missing Out

The signal to noise ratio (SNR) is an important consideration while designing an efficient engineering system – you need to maximize the signal and reduce the noise. Even if you can't increase the numerator, decreasing the denominator can still improve the overall ratio. Similarly, if you want to engineer a happy life, you must carefully find the right signals and separate them from noise. What are these signals and noises, though? There isn't a global definition, you have to find yours.

Broadly speaking, things that give you happiness are signals, ones that don't are noises. Same applies to people, not everyone in your life is a source of happiness or a positive influence. There should be *joy of missing out* (JOMO) these noises. Fear of missing out, if at all, should be reserved for signals.

JOMO, as compared to FOMO, is a step toward intentional living. For instance, if a certain networking event does not add value to your job, don't live in the fear of missing it. Instead, find joy in mindfully missing it. Accept that you can't visit all the pretty places, attend all the parties, watch all the movies, eat at all the restaurants. You can't be living a life based on someone else's Instagram feed, either. This incessant fear of missing out on perceived fun can soon spiral out, however joy by deliberating rejecting things that you don't want to do will amplify your happiness.

If you are confused about signals and noises in your life, a simple hack is to sleep over it. If something feels important even after ten hours, it is worth chasing. Also, know that your signals and noises will keep changing as you grow. Chances are erstwhile signals would become noises.

Driven by FOMO, we often waste our time doing things we don't enjoy. Most of us feel apologetic if we waste someone else's time, but we don't seem to have the same barometer for our own time. Fear snatches the control from us, joy gives it back. For a happy and satisfying life, our JOMO should always be greater than the FOMO.

Always remember, fear is temporary, joy is permanent. Choose wisely!

Seize the Day (Not a Myth)

Seize the Day, for Sure

Humans are obsessed with time. The moment we developed a basic understanding of the world around us, we started measuring time.

Humans overestimate time. Picture this: If you meet your parents once a year and they are sixty-five+, statistically speaking, you will meet them fifteen more times.

Humans underestimate time. We must not be scared to start our professional and personal lives all over again if we did it wrong the first time. But aren't we all?

Humans don't respect time. How else can you explain our daily habit of endless scrolling of the food images of a total stranger?

Humans can't enjoy time. Why do we feel guilty about wasting the time we loved wasting? Why do the hyper productive ones have to schedule every minute of every day?

Humans miscalculate time. We sacrifice our present by doing things we don't want to do, hoping we will get to do things we love to do in future. We wait for the perfect time to start living our best life.

Humans don't understand time. The only thing we want from time is for it to go back, and the only thing time does is move forward.

But, how is our happiness related to time? Give it *time*, we will come to it.

Time is as old and rigid as humanity itself. The concept kept evolving over time (pun intended) – some thirty thousand years ago the movements of our planet, sun, and moon were tracked to calculate time. Then, many natural phenomena like winds, rains, floods, the flowering of trees, migration of animals led to the concept of seasons. Subsequently, in the modern era, globalization led to the standardization of time. We know time as an entity that never stops. Time is a verb, noun and adjective for the world.

Even at a micro-level, our whole being is guided by time, it gives structure to our lives. A fixed number of hours make a day, a fixed number of days make a week, a fixed number of weeks make a year, and a fixed number of years make a life. We can't separate the quantification of time from our lives. It is all calculated. Even for one extra day, we have to wait for four long years. It is that rigid, that uniform.

Eventually though we all will run out of time, our time here is finite. We only have one lifetime, what are we saving it for? We must find the things that make us happy, and make time for them. The time we spend with a friend is not truly wasted, if it gives us happiness. It is not a race, we don't have to reach milestones at every age. We should earn the freedom to take control back of our time, but we don't require hyper accurate clocks or scheduling apps. We need to seize the day, every day.

Bonus Chapter: But, How Do You Cope with Bigger Problems Like Death?

Life goes on, till the time it doesn't. Where it ends, death starts. You move toward death inch by inch, every day; prepare for it all the time rather inadvertently; make several lists while living, trying to strike off most of the items in them, if not all. Every day though you are one step closer to death.

Death is an eventuality each one of us has to face, multiple times in our life. We can't escape it, it is inevitable not accidental. But when it hits you, when you lose someone, how prepared are you? How prepared can you possibly be? How can you think of ever being happy in the face of utter despair? You can't be. You just have to accept the nightmare, live through it and one day let your loved ones go from your memory. It's not that the dead abandons us, we abandon them too.

It is beyond the scope of this author's mind to suggest ways to cope up with death.

Conclusion: Happiness Needs No Justification

You don't have to explain your happiness, so long you are not breaking a law or harming yourself and/or others. The bottom line is to generate enough dopamine and endorphins. Whether they are generated by worldly pleasures, cerebral talks or a virtuous living, it does not matter. You may focus on momentarily enjoyment or lead a life of purpose or both. Virtue fails to guarantee happiness to everyone, hedonism is hardly the lock, stock and barrel of life. You can choose to follow Epicurus or Stoics[1] or both.

Understand and build your relationship with happiness, you neither have to intellectualize it, nor trivialize it. It is neither a reward, something that you necessarily deserve nor an impossible goal to achieve, something you have to spend all your energies on. You don't have to pressurize yourself to find happiness, and you don't have to feel guilty if you are happy. In fact, you don't even have to think about the definition of happiness, but the technique(s). Happiness does not have a universal definition, anyway. Just find what makes you happy, and hold on to it.

Make no mistake though, happiness is not about feeling good all the time, that is a herculean task. It is not even

---

[1] The Stoics cared about virtuous behavior and living according to nature, while the Epicureans were all about avoiding pain and seeking natural and necessary pleasure.

psychologically healthy. The state of excitement is followed by periods of lull, that's how physics (and life) works.

Both ecstasy and peace can be tenants in your happy life, sometimes oblivious to each other's presence, at other times existing in harmony. Just get on with that life, don't try to delineate it.
    Happiness needs no justification, for happiness in itself is enough.